Hillary Uses AI
to Plan Her
Hawaiian Vacation

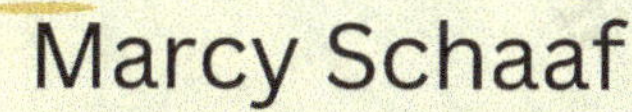

Marcy Schaaf

Copywrite @ 2024 Books By Schaaf Hillary
Uses AI to plan her Hawaiian Vacation

Hillary was buzzing with excitement—her family was finally going on a dream vacation to Hawaii! But planning such an epic trip?
That felt like solving a super-tough puzzle. There were so many questions running through her mind: What should they do? Where should they eat? How would they get around?

Luckily, Hillary had a secret weapon—AI! With just a few clever questions, Hillary could find all the answers she needed. From tasty Hawaiian snacks like Spam Musubi to fun activities for the whole family, AI was about to become her ultimate vacation planner.

Join Hillary as she uses AI to plan the perfect Hawaiian adventure, complete with sunshine, surfing, and of course, snacks!

Hillary loved technology
but she didn't love the questions in her brain.
So many!

Her family was going on vacation to Hawaii
and Hillary had BIG plans—mostly involving snacks.

"Al, what do kids in Hawaii eat?" she asked while doing her best hula dance. (It was more like a wiggly wave.)

Wi-Fi Calling
9:58 AM
ChatGPT
Kids in Hawaii often enjoy a mix of traditional Hawaiian foods, Asian-inspired dishes, and popular American fare. Some common foods include:
1. Spam Musubi – A snack made with rice, grilled Spam, and wrapped in seaweed, it's a favorite lunch or snack item.
2. Loco Moco – A local dish consisting of rice, a hamburger patty, a fried egg, and gravy on top.
3. Poke Bowls – Cubes of fresh raw fish (usually ahi tuna) marinated in soy sauce and sesame oil, often served with rice and various toppings.
4. Plate Lunch – A classic Hawaiian meal that includes rice, macaroni salad, and a meat like teriyaki beef, kalua pork, or chicken katsu.
Message

Hillary stared. "Spam... what now? Did you just sneeze?"

Al explained, "Spam Musubi! It's a snack made with Spam, rice, and seaweed. Super popular!"

"I've gotta try this!" Hillary declared.
"AI, can you find easy recipes so I don't accidentally set the kitchen on fire?"

Wi-Fi Calling
9:53 AM
google.com
Hawaiian Style Spam Musubi
9 ingredients · 1h 20m
Ono Hawaiia...
Spam Musubi
5.0 (753)
8 ingredients · 20m
NYT Cooking...
Barter-Worthy Spam Musubi
4.9 (106) · 7 ingredients · 45m
7

AI listed recipes and her mom immediately sighed.
"Great... Another rice explosions."

After a (slightly messy) cooking session
Hillary wanted more. "AI, what's a fun dessert?"

Al suggested,
"Shave ice is a Hawaiian favorite!
Try guava, li hing mui, or lychee flavors."

"Shave ice?!" Hillary grabbed a razor.
"Does it need a haircut?"

Her mom laughed and AI clarified
"No, it's just really fluffy ice with fruity syrup!"

Hillary slurped up her fruity creation.
"Oh wow, this is delicious!
I'm gonna eat shave ice every day in Hawaii!"

She also heard about a book called
Learn to Hula with Lani.
"AI, can you find this book?
My wiggly wave needs some serious help."

AI found the book and suggested,
"It's great for learning real hula dancing before your trip."

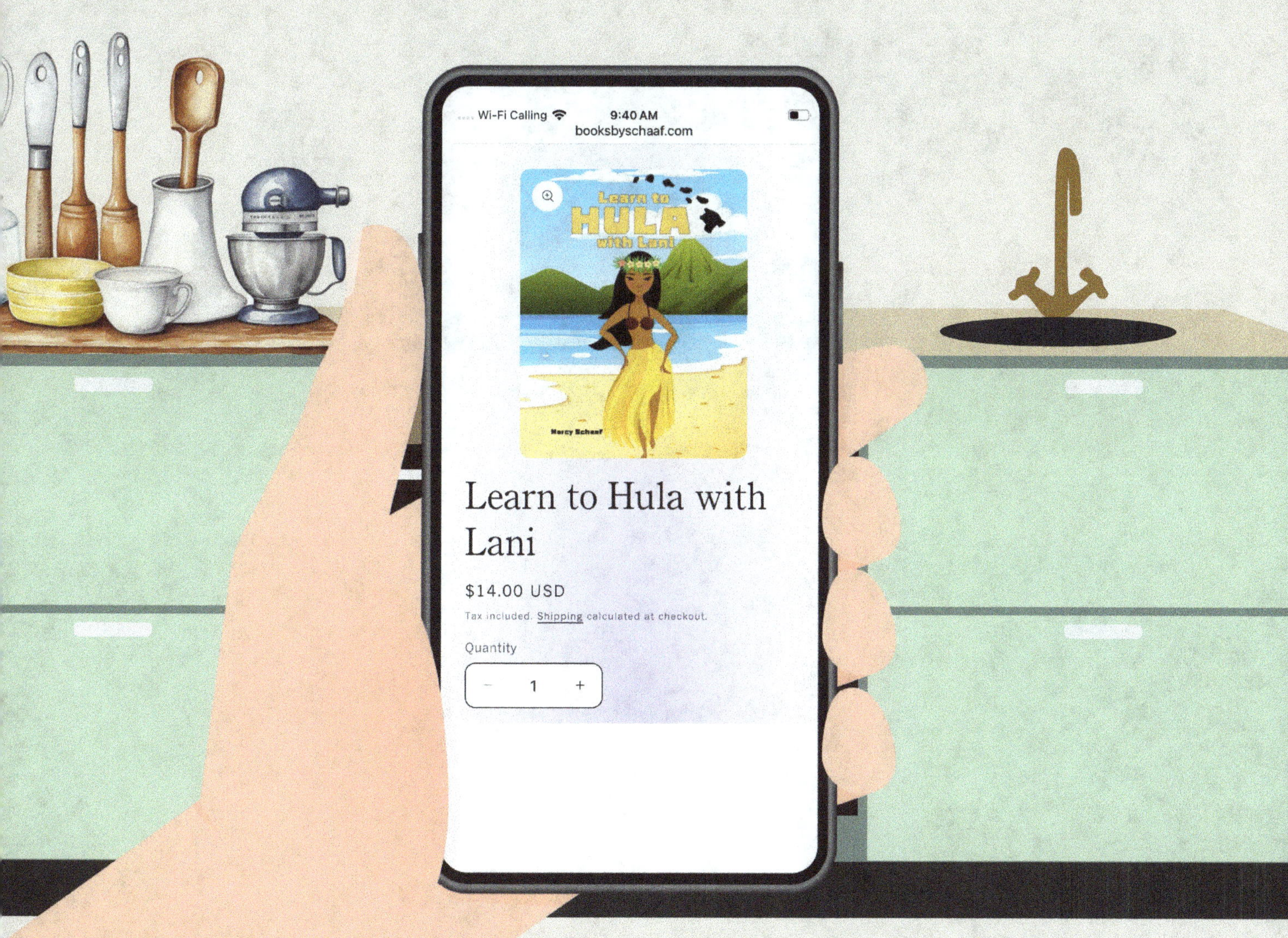

Hillary thought about all the fun things she could do in Hawaii. "AI, what are the best activities for kids? I'm thinking surfing, swimming, or maybe climbing a volcano!"

AI asked
"Do you want water adventures, hikes, or cultural events?
Or all three?"

"All three!" Hillary yelled
"And snacks in between, obviously."

Now, how far are these activities from the hotel?
"AI, how far is the volcano tour?"

AI responded
"It's 45 minutes away by car. Might wanna pack snacks."

Hillary grinned, "What about the bus?
Can I bring more snacks on the bus?"

AI replied, "Bus leaves every hour and stops five minutes from your hotel. And yes, you can bring snacks."

Dad asked, "How much is all this going to cost?"

AI responded,
"The tour costs $20 per person
and the public bus is FREE in Hawaii."

Hillary's dad sighed,
"$20 for volcanoes and bus. Not bad."

Hillary couldn't stop.
"AI, can you show me where the closest bus stop is to our hotel?"

Al mapped it out, and Hillary did a victory dance.
"It's right around the corner!"

"Now we can plan the whole day,"
Hillary said.
"AI, can you make me a snack-friendly route?"

Al suggested,
"Volcano tour, lunch near the beach, and then back on the bus with shave ice!"

Hillary cheered.
"This is the best vacation plan ever!
I'm gonna snack, surf, and see a volcano!"

Here's a simple recipe for Spam Musubi—a popular Hawaiian snack:

Ingredients:

1 can of Spam (regular or low-sodium)

3 cups of cooked sushi rice

3-4 sheets of nori (seaweed), cut in half

1/4 cup soy sauce

1/4 cup sugar

2 tablespoons rice vinegar (optional)

Instructions:

Cook the rice: Prepare sushi rice according to package instructions. Once cooked, let it cool slightly.

Slice the Spam: Cut the Spam into 8-10 slices.

Make the glaze: In a small pan, mix soy sauce and sugar over medium heat. Stir until the sugar dissolves.

Fry the Spam: Heat a non-stick skillet on medium heat and fry the Spam slices until golden on both sides. Pour the soy sauce glaze over the Spam and let it caramelize, turning the slices to coat evenly. Remove from heat.

Shape the rice: Wet your hands to prevent sticking and shape the rice into rectangular patties, roughly the same size as the Spam slices.

Assemble the musubi: Place a slice of Spam on top of each rice patty. Wrap the nori around the Spam and rice, using a bit of water to seal the edges of the seaweed.

Serve and enjoy: Let it cool slightly, and enjoy your homemade Spam Musubi!

Books By Schaaf

www.BookBySchaaf.com

Find us at:

Available at
amazon

BARNES & NOBLE

www.ingramcontent.com/pod-product-compliance
Lightning Source LLC
Chambersburg PA
CBHW081204130726
47996CB00009B/3237